MOUNT HOOD
portrait of a place

MOUNT HOOD
portrait of a place

PETER MARBACH

GRAPHIC ARTS BOOKS

To Lorena and Sofia, for your love and understanding of my passion for high places.
To my mother, Ethel, for the gifts of imagination, perseverance, and faith.
To all who cherish the mystery and grace of the mountain.

—PETER MARBACH

Photographs © MMVII by Peter Marbach

Library of Congress Control Number: 2006939026
International Standard Book Number: 978-0-88240-660-2

Captions and book compilation © MMVII by
Graphic Arts Books, an imprint of
Graphic Arts Center Publishing Company
P.O. Box 10306, Portland, Oregon 97296-0306
503/226-2402; www.gacpc.com

The five-dot logo is a registered trademark of
Graphic Arts Center Publishing Company.

President: Charles M. Hopkins
Associate Publisher: Douglas A. Pfeiffer
Editorial Staff: Timothy W. Frew, Kathy Howard, Jean Bond-Slaughter
Production Coordinator: Heather Doornink
Cover Design: Elizabeth Watson
Interior Design: Jean Andrews

Printed in China

FRONT COVER: ◖ Vine maple at
Lost Lake frames Mount Hood in fall colors.
BACK COVER: ◖ Wildflowers carpet a hillside at Compass Creek.
◄◄ At Timothy Lake, a quiet day of fishing offers restoration. Fish in
the lake include kokanee, eastern brook, rainbow and cutthroat trout.
◄ Wy'east, the legendary chief of the Multnomah tribe, reveals his face
and headdress near the North Face summit of Mount Hood. Only when
snow and light conditions are just right is it possible to see his features.
► From the Pittock Mansion at dawn, the silhouette of Mount
Hood looms beyond the lights of the city of Portland.

◄ This unnamed waterfall at Cast Creek was only discovered a few
years ago. With no trail leading to it, getting there is pure bushwhacking—
actually walking in the stream for a few miles—but it's worth the effort!
▲ Salmon may migrate several thousand miles into the salty waters of the sea
from the time they leave the freshwater rivers as juveniles until they
return as adults. Here, salmon return to spawn in Eagle Creek.

▲ Warm light bathes the Sandy River. Named the
Quicksand River by the Lewis and Clark Expedition,
the name was later shortened simply to the Sandy. The
2,650-mile Pacific Crest Trail crosses here as it wends
its way from the Mexican border to Canada.

▲ An early morning sunburst lights up the
rim of the Devils Kitchen Headwall near the summit
of Mount Hood. The headwall is near the Steel Cliffs, to
the east of the Hogsback, a popular climbing route
that leads to the pinnacle of the mountain.

▲ Many miles of hiking trails are maintained on the mountain. At
Alder Flat, the trail winds through old-growth forest and lush undergrowth.
▶ Rhododendron almost seem out of place where only forest is expected.
Here their delicate color accents Douglas-firs near Marco Creek.

▲ In 1910, at the 8,600-foot level on the upper reaches of Cooper Spur, this rock was carved as a monument to a successful climb of Mount Hood. According to the inscription, the two climbers were Takahashi from Japan's Hiroshima Prefecture and Itoh from the Mie Prefecture.

► The cascading waters of Ramona Falls make it a popular destination for day trips. The volume of water is actually less than one might expect, but this waterfall fans out to a wide base, creating a stunning display.

◄ Though not as well-known as skiing,
dog sledding is popular on the mountain. This
musher is enjoying a day with his dogs near Frog Lake.
▲ The Palmer Snowfield attracts thousands
of skiers for summer play.

▲ Swirling snow seems to be trying to make
its own funnel cloud above the Salmon River
Canyon. The difference between blowing snow and
clouds is sometimes nearly impossible to discern.

▲ Fireweed seedpods glisten in afternoon sun
near McGee Creek. The plant is one of the first to
move into cleared or burned-off woodlands.

▲ Built by the Civilian Conservation Corps in 1934, this wooden
shelter at Elk Meadows is one of the last such shelters on the Timberline Trail.
▶ An unusual volcanic formation stands near Routson Park in Mount Hood National Forest.
▶▶ Water from the Laurance Lake settling pond helps irrigate the upper Hood
River Valley. The pond is the site of an annual kids' fishing derby.

◀ First light bathes white park pine krummholz high along the Texas Trails
at Mount Hood Meadows. Though the word *krummholz* has several uses, here
it refers to the matlike surface of pine remnants on exposed ridges above tree line.
▲ Star trails overhead and a glowing campfire near Cloud Cap Inn show why
so many enjoy camping in the Mount Hood National Forest. With no
distracting city lights, the heavens seem close enough to touch.

▲ A lush carpet of purple-hued lupine, interspersed with occasional bright red paintbrush, covers an alpine meadow at Elk Cove.

▶ On their first backpacking trip ever, students from Springwater Trail High School in Gresham enjoy the view from the Dollar Lake campsite.

◀ At 4:00 A.M. moonset lights the
snow-dusted streets of Government Camp.
▲ At dawn, the waters of Eliot Creek evoke feelings of
drama and power, peace and tranquillity. Eliot Creek,
which starts as meltwater from Eliot Glacier, flows
into the Middle Fork of the Hood River.

▲ In the Columbia Wilderness Area, Eagle Creek
receives Metlako Falls. The first major waterfall encountered
along the Eagle Creek Trail, Metlako Falls is also the highest at 130 feet.
► The Columbia River Gorge is a world-class site for windsurfing: the
westward-flowing Columbia River is counterbalanced much of the
year by east winds, creating ideal windsurfing conditions.

◄ Near Vista Ridge, the setting sun backlights
blooming bear grass, *Xerophyllum tenax*. Although
bear grass looks like a grass, it is actually part of the lily family.
The plant grows from about four and a half feet high to six feet high.
▲ Part of the Mount Hood Complex Wildland Fire of 2006, the
Bluegrass Ridge fire burns along the west side of Highway 35.

▲ A fisherman enjoys the pristine waters of
the Salmon River. In addition to fishing, there
are many ways to earn solitude: backpacking,
kayaking, and camping, to name just a few.

▲ The West Fork of the Hood River reveals
columns of basalt rock, the result of cooled basaltic lava.
Basaltic lava can flow quickly, moving several miles from
a vent. Basalt is earth's most common type of rock.

▲ Timberline Trail, a forty-mile path that circles Mount Hood,
passes by a waterfall adorned with lupine, paintbrush, and cow parsnip.
▶ A weathered pine remnant graces a windy ridge at McNeil Point.
▶▶ Haloed by a lenticular cloud, the mountain stands
high above a pasture near Parkdale.

▲ From a tarn near the Langille Glacier, Jerry Bryan takes in a view
of Mount Adams, which lies across the Columbia River in Washington
some thirty miles east of Mount St. Helens. Adams has a height of 12,276 feet.
► Purple lupine softens harsh rock edges in the boulder-strewn Cairn Basin,
near Vista Ridge on the remote northwest side of the mountain.

◄ A single avalanche lily brightens Wy'east
Basin. As soon as the snow melts, avalanche lilies
carpet the forest floor with their delicate blossoms.
▲ Wildflowers blanket a meadow at Paradise Park,
picking up and repeating the pastel colors
of the mountain above at day's end.

▲ A 1930s Works Progress Administration (WPA) project,
Timberline Lodge was constructed at the 6,600-foot level on Mount
Hood. The lodge was dedicated in 1937 by President Franklin D. Roosevelt.
► Glacial ice looms high above the headwaters of Newton Creek.

◄ Nestled beneath the mountain,
Trillium Lake draws a solitary kayaker to its serene
beauty. To guard the tranquillity, no motors are allowed on the lake.
▲ Paintbrush scatters its brilliance at Mount Hood Meadows.

◄ Snow and ice encase the Sahalie Falls, creating a winter wonderland.
▲ A vine maple leaf rests on early fall snow near Laurance Lake. Vine maple
is one of Oregon's most colorful trees, turning brilliant red in fall.

▲ Timberline Lodge is the site for numerous mountain- and snow-
related activities—among them, summer snowboarding competitions.
► Recreationists going to Timothy and Olallie lakes often stop by the
Clackamas Lake Historic Ranger Station near Timothy Lake. The ranger
station offers information as well as tours of the historic facility.

◄ Climbers on the South Side route to the summit of
Mount Hood traverse the Hogsback. More than ten thousand
climbers register to climb to Hood's 11,239-foot peak each year.
▲ With a seventy-inch wingspan and a thirty-eight-inch length, a great
blue heron *(Ardea herodias)* patiently waits for fish at Eagle Creek. Its
gray-blue coloring, long legs, and large bill are distinguishing features.

◀ Scarlet vine maple contrasts with the
dark gray lava rock in the sprawling expanse of the
Lava Beds Geologic Area near Parkdale. The area's eruptive
history dates from 7,500 years to just 250 years ago.
▲ A spotlight of sun illuminates a trillium
near Summit Prairie Meadows.

▲ Since 1992, the number of wineries
in Oregon has more than tripled, making the
growing of wine grapes, such as these at Carabella Vineyard in
the Willamette Valley, a major segment of the state's agricultural product.
► Near the town of Wasco, in Sherman County, a grain elevator rises
amidst wheat fields. The farming area grows mostly wheat and barley.

◄ Winter blankets the White River at the White River Sno-Park.
▲ Crag Rats ascend the Snow Dome in search of a missing climber. Founded
in 1926, the all-volunteer Crag Rats are among the first to respond to
an emergency on the mountain, as well as in the Columbia
River Gorge and throughout the surrounding area.

▲ Fall colors, clouds, and mist soften the lines of
both the actual Mount Hood and its reflection in Lost Lake, a
deep, clear, freshwater lake covering almost three hundred surface acres.
► A hiker enjoys the view along the historic Barlow Road, built in 1846.
►► Sunrise burns through fog over the White River. Beginning in
the Mount Hood National Forest, the river flows some forty-
seven miles to its confluence with the Deschutes River.

◄ Cottonwood and golden larch line the East Fork of Hood River.
▲ A grouse's natural camouflage enables it to blend quite nicely with
the rocky terrain near the Langille Crags, which rise just east of the
Langille Glacier. The crags and the glacier were named for the
family that first operated Cloud Cap Inn in the 1890s.

▲ Kerosene smudge pots protect a
pear crop from freezing temperatures.
► Pear blossoms frame Mount Hood in the Hood
River Valley. Hood River County is the number
one pear-growing county in the nation.

◄ Fall colors along Forest Service Road 48 on the way to Bonney
Butte include greens and golds along with the vibrant red of vine maple—
backdropped by the ever-looming snow-covered peak of Mount Hood.
▲ Andesite outcroppings above 15 Mile Creek evoke images of other-
worldly stone creatures just waiting to be brought to life.

▲ The banks of the East Fork of Hood River are
free of snow only a few months of the year. The East Fork,
about fifteen miles long, is fed by glacial runoff from Mount Hood.
▶ Sunset light silhouettes the mountain against a brilliant sky.

◄ A trail curves behind the Tamanawas Falls, enabling one to
feel the power and mist. The falls' hundred-foot drop can be reached
by a hike of just a couple of miles off Highway 35 on Mount Hood's east side.
▲ Oaks frame the confluence of the West and East forks of the Hood River.
Originating on Mount Hood, the Hood River merges with the Columbia
River twenty-two miles upstream of the Bonneville Dam.

71

▲ Wintery winds swirl over the Barrett Spur, 7,850 feet in elevation.

▶ The luminous gold of larch trees near the Badger Creek Wilderness frames a
mountain "hooded" by a lenticular cloud. The Badger Creek Wilderness
encompasses some fifty-five miles of trails, including the Badger Creek
National Recreation Trail, which stretches the length of the creek
in the wilderness, a distance of nearly twelve miles.

◄ A hiker enjoys a view of Reid Glacier from the Yocum Ridge Trail.
▲ An elk herd of between two- and three thousand ranges in the Mount Hood
National Forest. Roosevelt elk usually roam west of the Cascades; Rocky Mountain elk,
to the east. Roosevelt elk are larger and darker than Rocky Mountain elk; their antlers,
shorter and heavier. The two varieties often mix to form the Mount Hood herd.
►► Sunlight bursts through morning fog near Tilly Jane Campground.

◄ The Salmon River's headwaters rise near Timberline Lodge.
▲ The stern-wheeler *Columbia Gorge* carries swimmers to Hood River
for the annual Roy Webster Columbia River Cross Channel Swim. The
stern-wheeler runs day cruises on the Willamette and the Columbia.

▲ Open fairways and hilly terrain—and, of course, views
of Mount Hood—are all hallmarks of Gresham's Persimmon Country
Club. Not as well-known is the fact that in places on the well-kept grounds
three other mountains are visible: Mounts St. Helens, Jefferson, and Adams.
► The main branch of the Hood River flows with white-water swiftness
near the Apple Valley Country Store. Three major forks
combine to make up the mainstream Hood River.

◄ Kingsley Reservoir is a popular site for a number of recreational activities, including
mountain biking, fishing, and swimming. One event, the Mountain Man Off-Road Festival, includes
both a Triathlon and a Half Marathon; both competitions begin and end at the Kingsley Reservoir.
▲ A deer ventures into a clearing at Mitchell Point. Several tunnels were cut through Mitchell Point
as part of the Historic Columbia River Highway, the only highway through the Columbia River
Gorge on the Oregon side before construction of Interstate 84, completed in 1980.

▲ Crevasses, deep fissures in the
glacier ice, form patterns at Eliot Glacier.
► Towering seracs show the power inherent in Eliot Glacier.
The most studied of the mountain's glaciers, Eliot faces
Hood River, on the mountain's northeast slope.

▲ A collage of bright reds and greens
accents the autumn forest near Dog River Trail.
► Scattered across the ground, leaves of a brilliant
red vine maple partner with tree roots to create an
intricate design at the Sherwood Campground.

◄ A fisherman enjoys the solitude of Mirror
Lake. The area around the lake is also a favorite for
hiking, especially on weekends from June through October.
▲ Moonlight illuminates a sulphur vent in the fumarole fields near
Crater Rock. An active volcano, Mount Hood's most recent eruption
was shortly before Lewis and Clark's 1805 Expedition.

▲ A springtime aerial of the North Face of Mount Hood
reveals 10,497-foot Mount Jefferson forty miles to the south.

► Clark Creek flows through Heather Canyon. Towering above the
canyon, Mount Hood sets off the rushing creek and the steep canyon walls.

►► Little Crater Lake's clear waters come from a natural artesian spring.
Less than one hundred feet across, the lake is forty-five feet deep.

▲ Smoke from a forest fire intensifies a sunset view of Mount St. Helens across
the Columbia River in Washington. The May 18, 1980, eruption of Mount St. Helens blew
some 1,300 feet off the top of the mountain, bringing its present elevation to 8,364 feet.
► Julio Viamonte enjoys telemark skiing on Cooper Spur. Originating in Norway,
telemark skiing is distinguished by a technique for making turns.
Cooper Spur is on the majestic north side of the mountain.

◄ Children (without wings) fly down the alpine slide at Sky Bowl.
▲ A skier jumps over a corniced ridge on the Palmer Glacier, on the
upper slopes of Mount Hood. Palmer, a remnant of massive
glaciers that formed during the last ice age, is the best
known of the mountain's eleven glaciers.

▲ A family skis in to the picturesque Summit
Meadow Cabins, located near Government Camp, for a
weekend of rest, relaxation, and recreation.

▲ A snow bridge forms a tunnel over the Zigzag River. Obviously,
care is needed: what looks like a solid place to stand may not be safe at all.
▶▶ On a calm spring evening, lights from the Hood River/White
Salmon Interstate Bridge are reflected in the Columbia River.

▲ A sunset view from the Magic Mile lift
above Timberline Lodge yields a vista of unending
ridges and valleys stretching off into the distance. The first
Magic Mile was built in 1938; the second, in 1962; and the third
(and present) lift was constructed in 1992. As its name might
indicate, the lift is presently just over a mile in length.

▲ The Flag Point forest fire lookout, in
the Barlow Ranger District, is available for rentals from
November through May. The present lookout, constructed in
1973 and replacing the original one built around 1924,
still serves in summer as a working fire lookout.

▲ Evening light creates a romantic setting at the historic
Cloud Cap Inn, built in 1889. Situated at the 6,000-foot elevation on the
northeast shoulder of Mount Hood, Cloud Cap averages sixty *feet* of snow each winter.
▶ Condos at Collins Lake Resort signal development at Government Camp. In fall 1849, mounted
riflemen headed to Oregon City over the Barlow Road. Bad weather forced them to abandon a
number of cavalry wagons beside the trail, thus inspiring the name *Government Camp*.

◄ A stone shelter gives comfort
for skiers and climbers at Cooper Spur.
▲ Snow turns a boulder field into a winter moonscape
in the White River basin. The glacier-fed White
River flows off the east side of Mount Hood.

◄ A crescent moon rises over Ski Bowl, America's
largest nighttime ski area, located at Government Camp.
▲ A pine snag frames a fiery winter sunset
over Timberline Lodge.

▲ Crag Rats, an elite search and rescue group, practice climbing out of
a crevasse. The nation's oldest mountain search and rescue organization,
the Crag Rats are charter members of the Mountain Rescue Association.
► The moon sets over Illumination Rock, on the mountain's southwest side.
In 1845, desperate to reach the Willamette Valley before winter, Joel
Palmer climbed to Illumination Rock to scout an overland route.
►► A climber celebrates reaching the summit of Mount Hood.